Mapping Common Worship

Mind Maps [illegible] Your Way Round All the Volu[illegible]rship

Phili[illegible]

Director of Licensed Lay Minister Training, Diocese of Oxford and
Tutor in Liturgy, Ripon College, Cuddesdon

GROVE BOOKS LIMITED
RIDLEY HALL RD CAMBRIDGE CB3 9HU

Contents

Acknowledgments

I want to thank Trevor Lloyd and Peter Moger for making many helpful suggestions and pointing me to the right material. This exercise was more complex than I anticipated at the beginning. I also want to thank James Blandford-Baker for his work in the production of the maps. This also was a rather difficult operation.

'Transforming Worship: Living the New Creation' is the logo of the Church of England Liturgical Commission's initiative in liturgical formation. Launched in July 2007, it seeks to encourage and enable good practice in the leading and preparation of worship. The initiative involves the Commission working with many organisations through the church, of which Grove Books and the Group for the Renewal of Worship are major partners.

The Cover Illustration is by Peter Ashton

First Impression April 2008

ISSN 0144-1728

ISBN 978 1 85174 684 2

1 Why an Overview?

Common Worship has been a radical change in Church of England worship.

Once centred round a single book, the *Book of Common Prayer*, worship is now a number of volumes, twelve in all. The purpose of this book is to give an overview of this official provision.

In the past it was a simple affair to open the *Prayer Book* to find what was needed. This is now more complex.[1] The mind maps in this book include all the Common Worship volumes. They give an overview of each volume indicating the services included. The maps start in the top right hand corner and should be read clockwise. They are printed on one page each in this book. On the opposite page is a brief introduction to the volume; further bibliographical material is on the supporting Grove Books web page.

The maps indicate a certain amount of overlap between the volumes. But many resources are only found in particular volumes, for example musical settings for the eucharistic prayers are only in the *President's Edition* and *Festivals*. The maps try to indicate this and guide you to the right volume to finding the service you want.

Common Worship includes two types of resources, that which is authorized and that which is commended. Authorized material has gone through a process of revision in General Synod and is alternative to the *Book of Common Prayer*. It is indicative of the doctrine and practice of the Church of England and leaders are quite limited in the changes that can be made to that text. Commended material is approved by the House of Bishops and has a lesser status; it can be more freely adapted for local use. It is important to grasp this difference and to be clear which worship texts are in which category. In Common Worship some volumes contain large amounts of authorized material others have comparatively small amounts.

Thus Common Worship is a rich resource to help congregations worship God in Christ through the Spirit.

2 Services and Prayers for the Church of England—the Main Volume

One early decision on Common Worship was that the main volume would be for the Sunday Services, Principal Feasts and Holy Days of the church.

It might have helped if this volume were more clearly labelled as some people have mistakenly viewed this volume as the definitive book, with other books as supplementary. This missed the point of there being a series of volumes rather than one main book. These volumes are called 'a collection of services' in the preface.

This book contains a mixture of services any parish might use on a Sunday including Morning and Evening Prayer from the *Book of Common Prayer*. There are also services from *Christian Initiation*. This book is perhaps mostly used for the services of Holy Communion and is the volume where most of the material for Holy Communion is found, but not everything. As *Common Worship Additional Collects* was produced later, they are not found in this book, but either in the offprint or in *Common Worship Collects and Post Communions*. Communion by Extension was deliberately not included in this volume to indicate its extra-ordinary status.

Texts

The Archbishops' Council, *Common Worship: Services and Prayers for the Church of England* (London: CHP, 2000)

The Archbishops' Council, *Common Worship: Additional Collects* (London: CHP, 2004)

The Archbishops' Council, *Common Worship: Collects and Post Communions* (London: CHP, 2004)

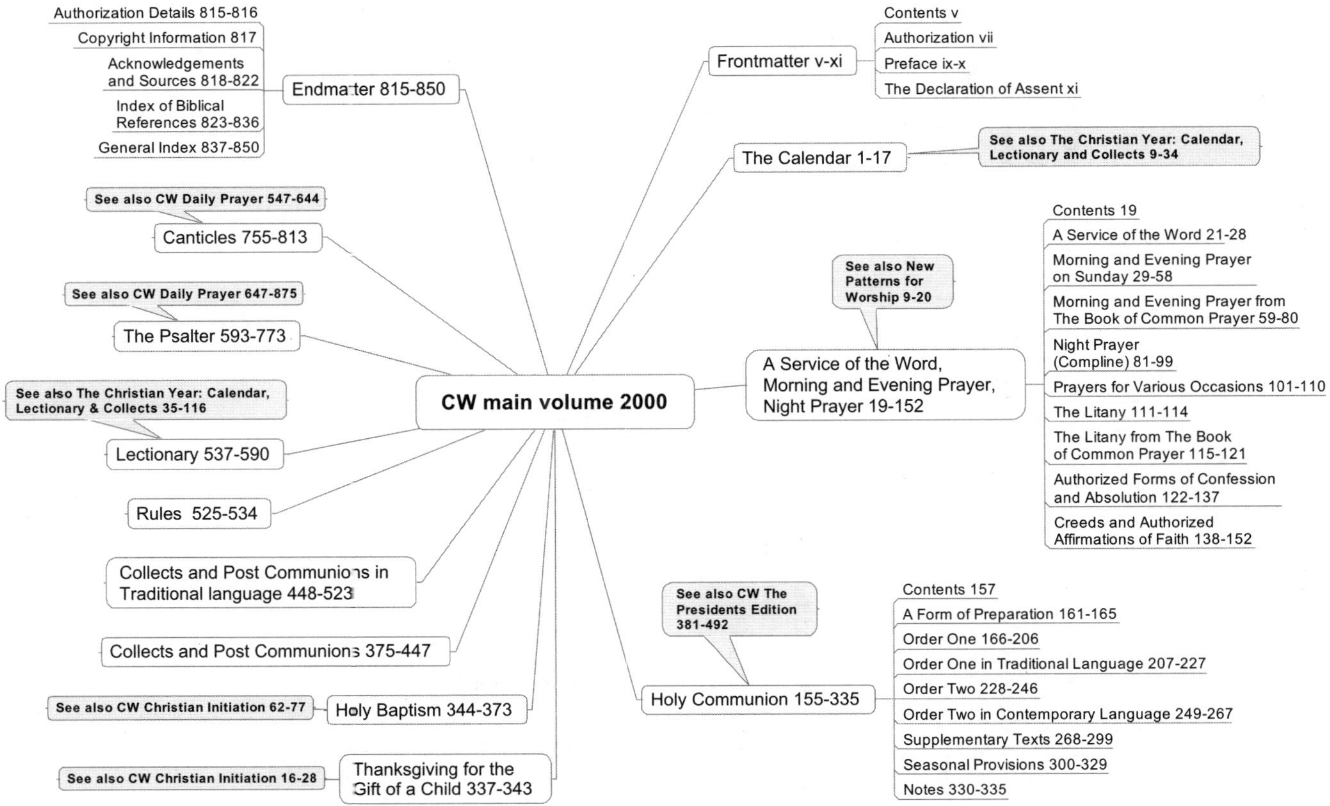
CW main volume 2000
Frontmatter v-xi
Contents v
Authorization vii
Preface ix-x
The Declaration of Assent xi
The Calendar 1-17
See also The Christian Year: Calendar, Lectionary and Collects 9-34
A Service of the Word, Morning and Evening Prayer, Night Prayer 19-152
See also New Patterns for Worship 9-20
Contents 19
A Service of the Word 21-28
Morning and Evening Prayer on Sunday 29-58
Morning and Evening Prayer from The Book of Common Prayer 59-80
Night Prayer (Compline) 81-99
Prayers for Various Occasions 101-110
The Litany 111-114
The Litany from The Book of Common Prayer 115-121
Authorized Forms of Confession and Absolution 122-137
Creeds and Authorized Affirmations of Faith 138-152
Holy Communion 155-335
See also CW The Presidents Edition 381-492
Contents 157
A Form of Preparation 161-165
Order One 166-206
Order One in Traditional Language 207-227
Order Two 228-246
Order Two in Contemporary Language 249-267
Supplementary Texts 268-299
Seasonal Provisions 300-329
Notes 330-335
Thanksgiving for the Gift of a Child 337-343
See also CW Christian Initiation 16-28
Holy Baptism 344-373
See also CW Christian Initiation 62-77
Collects and Post Communions 375-447
Collects and Post Communions in Traditional language 448-523
Rules 525-534
Lectionary 537-590
See also The Christian Year: Calendar, Lectionary & Collects 35-116
The Psalter 593-773
See also CW Daily Prayer 647-875
Canticles 755-813
See also CW Daily Prayer 547-644
Endmatter 815-850
Authorization Details 815-816
Copyright Information 817
Acknowledgements and Sources 818-822
Index of Biblical References 823-836
General Index 837-850

3 The President's Edition

This volume is designed as a book for the president to use.

It contains much of what is in the main book, but is designed for use in presiding at Communion. For this reason there are various resources here not found in the Sunday book, such as music for the eucharistic prayers, and some additional seasonal material including collects for lesser feast days in traditional language. The order of the material is also different to enable the centre of the book to be the main eucharistic material. The cost of the book means that many churches have not purchased a copy but use locally customized or printed books.

As well as the additional material not found elsewhere, this volume also includes material from other volumes but not in the main volume such as the eucharistic prefaces for pastoral services, marriage and baptism. So it is not simply a larger print version of the main volume but has a different rationale.

There seem to be no specific commentaries on this edition. However, the overlap with the Sunday book provides much commentary material. There was in 1997 a major report on the theology of presidency produced by the House of Bishops. This is in part in light of an ongoing debate on lay presidency. There are some helpful resources on presidency and leading worship, which are provided on the Grove website.

Text

The Archbishops' Council, *Common Worship: President's Edition* (London: CHP, 2000)

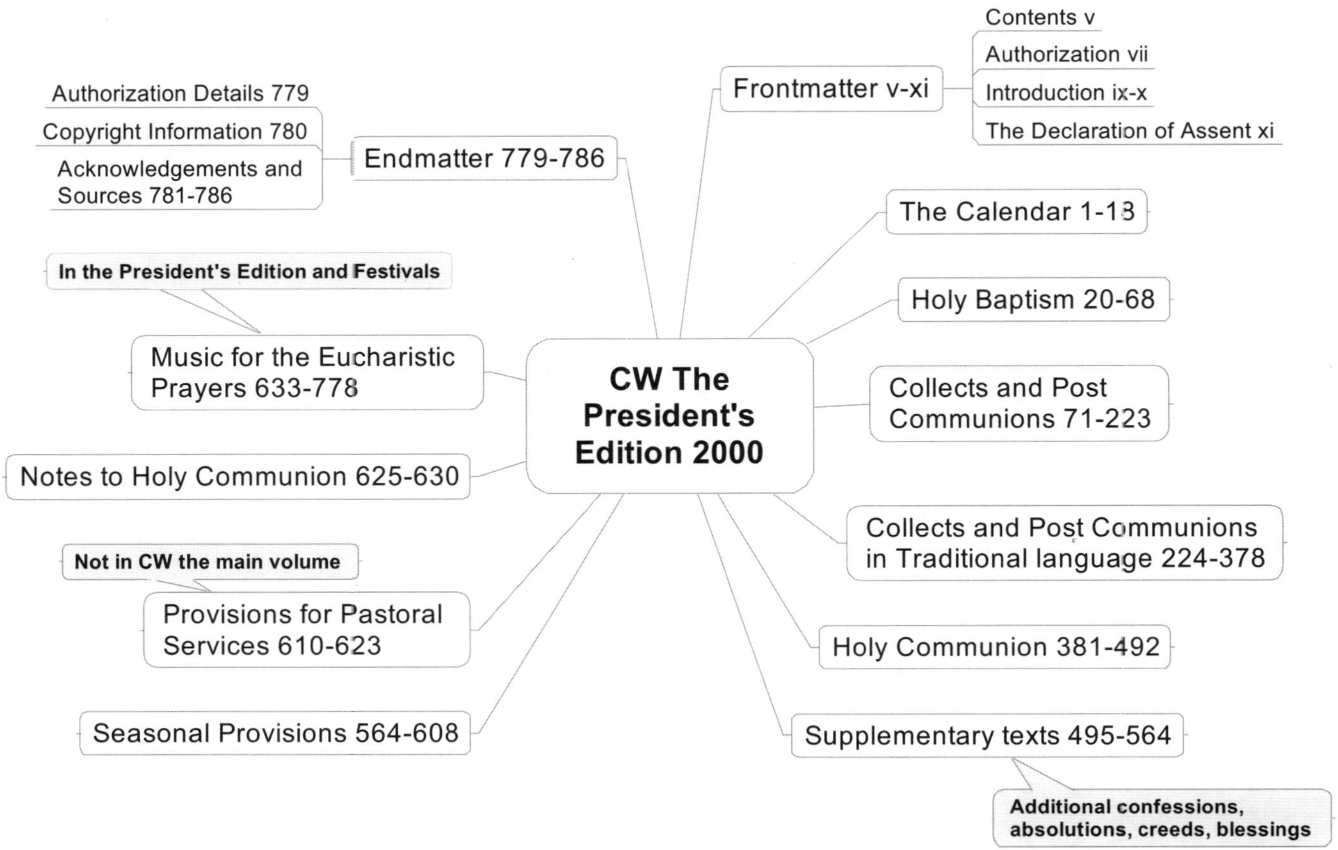
CW The President's Edition 2000
Frontmatter v-xi
Contents v
Authorization vii
Introduction ix-x
The Declaration of Assent xi
The Calendar 1-13
Holy Baptism 20-68
Collects and Post Communions 71-223
Collects and Post Communions in Traditional language 224-378
Holy Communion 381-492
Supplementary texts 495-564
Additional confessions, absolutions, creeds, blessings
Seasonal Provisions 564-608
Provisions for Pastoral Services 610-623
Not in CW the main volume
Notes to Holy Communion 625-630
Music for the Eucharistic Prayers 633-778
In the President's Edition and Festivals
Endmatter 779-786
Authorization Details 779
Copyright Information 780
Acknowledgements and Sources 781-786

4 Christian Initiation

Christian Initiation (2006) had a predecessor, Initiation Services (1998).

The latter was a work in progress leading to the fuller material of the 2006 book. As one of the first volumes in Common Worship, *Initiation Services* (1998) received considerable criticism and schedules of amendments were introduced in 2000 and 2005. These have now been incorporated into *Christian Initiation* along with material from other volumes and new material. *Christian Initiation* replaces *Initiation Services* although there is a large overlap of material. Both volumes include helpful official commentaries, which are important to read. Both point back to *On the Way* (1995) as a key report of the House of Bishops in developing the theology and missiological strategy behind the liturgical texts. *Christian Initiation* acknowledges the vital contribution of Michael Vasey to these reports. On an international Anglican level the IALC Toronto Statement is an important background document.

Texts

The Archbishops' Council, *Common Worship: Christian Initiation* (London: CHP, 2006)

The Central Board of Finance of the Church of England, *Common Worship: Initiation Services* (London: CHP, 1997, 1998)

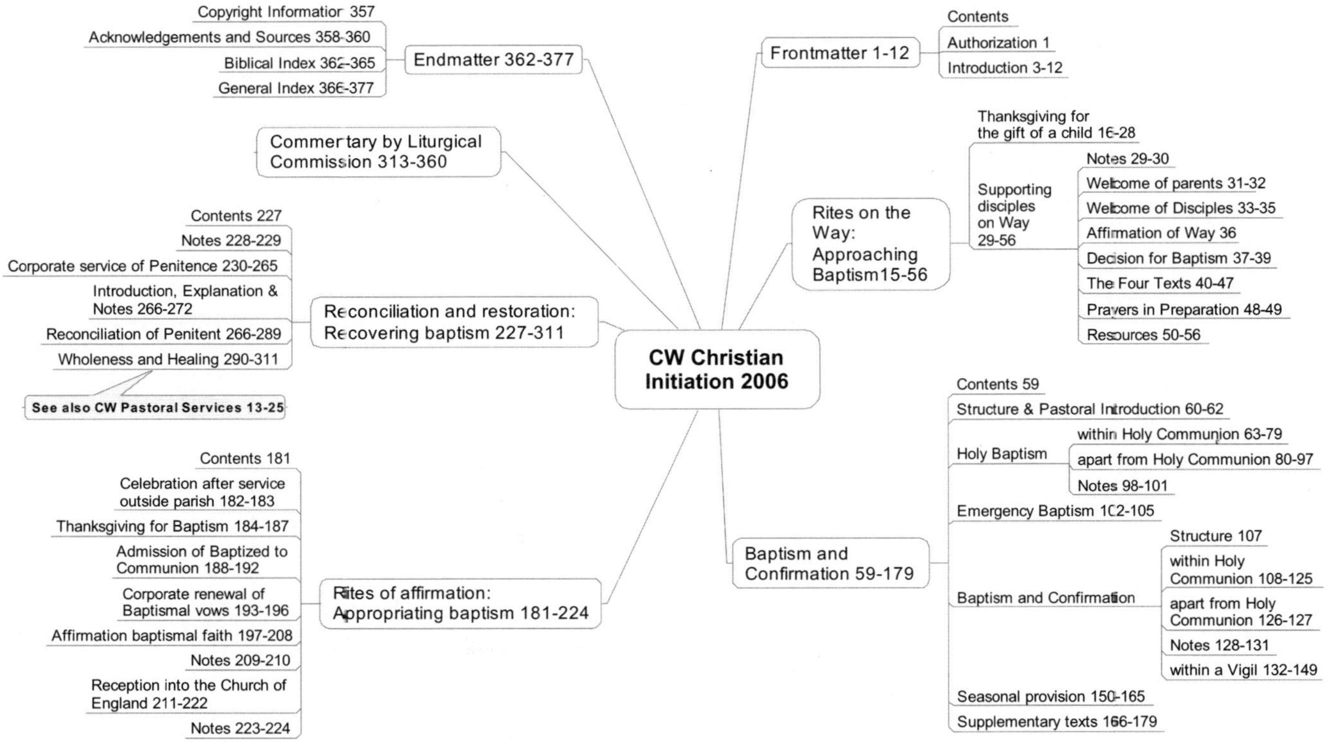
CW Christian Initiation 2006
Frontmatter 1-12
Contents
Authorization 1
Introduction 3-12
Rites on the Way: Approaching Baptism15-56
Thanksgiving for the gift of a child 16-28
Supporting disciples on Way 29-56
Notes 29-30
Welcome of parents 31-32
Welcome of Disciples 33-35
Affirmation of Way 36
Decision for Baptism 37-39
The Four Texts 40-47
Prayers in Preparation 48-49
Resources 50-56
Baptism and Confirmation 59-179
Contents 59
Structure & Pastoral Introduction 60-62
Holy Baptism
within Holy Communion 63-79
apart from Holy Communion 80-97
Notes 98-101
Emergency Baptism 102-105
Baptism and Confirmation
Structure 107
within Holy Communion 108-125
apart from Holy Communion 126-127
Notes 128-131
within a Vigil 132-149
Seasonal provision 150-165
Supplementary texts 166-179
Endmatter 362-377
Copyright Informatior 357
Acknowledgements and Sources 358-360
Biblical Index 362-365
General Index 366-377
Commer tary by Liturgical Commission 313-360
Reconciliation and restoration: Recovering baptism 227-311
Contents 227
Notes 228-229
Corporate service of Penitence 230-265
Introduction, Explanation & Notes 266-272
Reconciliation of Penitent 266-289
Wholeness and Healing 290-311
See also CW Pastoral Services 13-25
Rites of affirmation: Appropriating baptism 181-224
Contents 181
Celebration after service outside parish 182-183
Thanksgiving for Baptism 184-187
Admission of Baptized to Communion 188-192
Corporate renewal of Baptismal vows 193-196
Affirmation baptismal faith 197-208
Notes 209-210
Reception into the Church of England 211-222
Notes 223-224

5 Pastoral Services

Pastoral Services comes in two editions.

The second in 2005 added the Alternative Services Series One of Matrimony and Funerals to the book, giving traditional language services to the volume.

The volume is a rich set of resources of healing, marriage and funerals. Healing has been a growing part of the church's ministry, both through the charismatic movement and in more traditional circles. A major report *A Time to Heal* (2000) discussed the healing ministry in great fullness, and tried to set out some guidelines for good practice. There are many other excellent books commending the healing ministry.

Marriage has been much discussed in the church with reports about the family and remarriage of divorced persons. There are also ongoing debates about the legal context. Funerals services are now rich in their provision. The Joint Liturgical Group produces the service book used in many crematoria that includes Common Worship provision alongside Roman Catholic and Free Church services.

Pastoral services have been revised considering the best pastoral practice in light of developments in pastoral psychology and taking into consideration the 'rites of passage' model developed in anthropology. The material is rich and needs careful selection to fit the occasion.

Texts

The Archbishops' Council, *Common Worship: Pastoral Services* (2nd ed, London: CHP, 2005)

JLG, *Funeral Services of the Christian Churches of England* (3rd revised ed, Norwich: Canterbury Press, 2001)

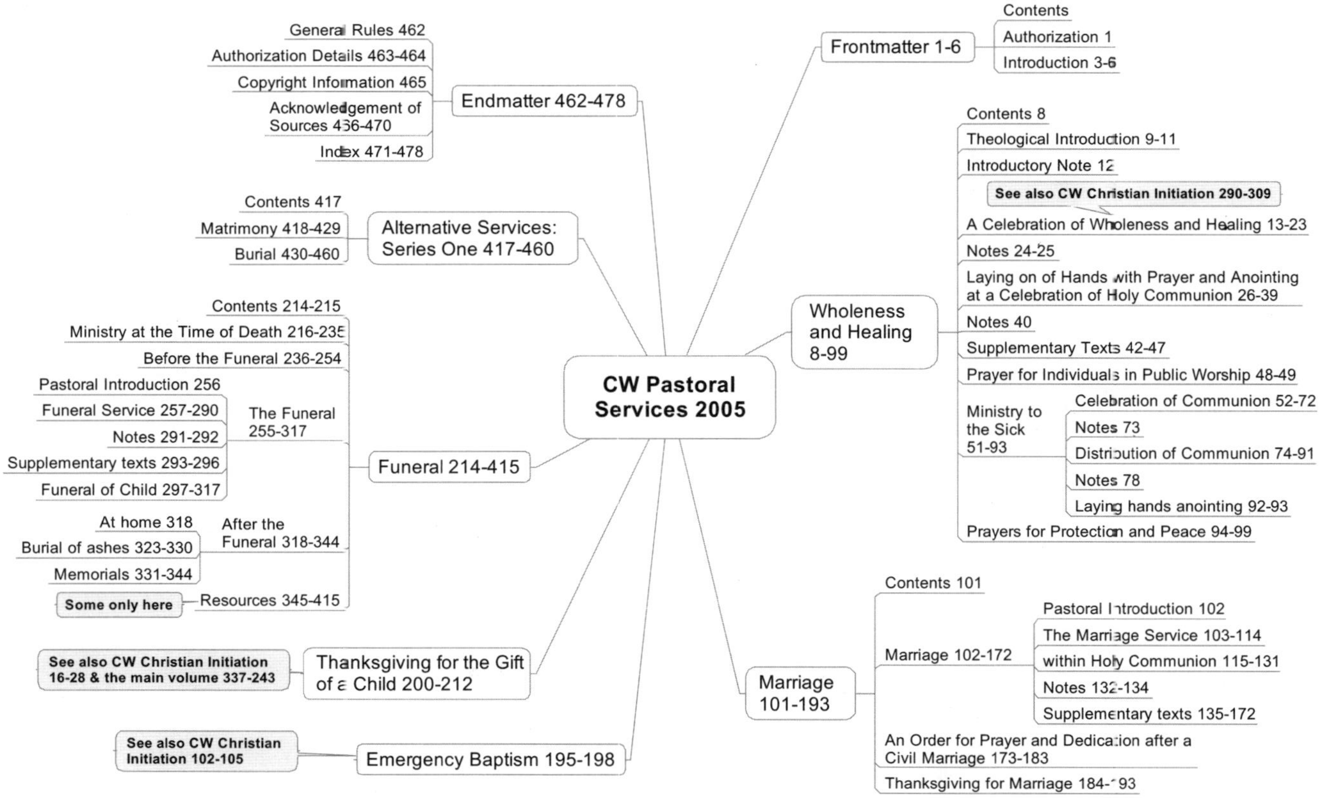
CW Pastoral Services 2005
Frontmatter 1-6
Contents
Authorization 1
Introduction 3-6
Wholeness and Healing 8-99
Contents 8
Theological Introduction 9-11
Introductory Note 12
See also CW Christian Initiation 290-309
A Celebration of Wholeness and Healing 13-23
Notes 24-25
Laying on of Hands with Prayer and Anointing at a Celebration of Holy Communion 26-39
Notes 40
Supplementary Texts 42-47
Prayer for Individuals in Public Worship 48-49
Ministry to the Sick 51-93
Celebration of Communion 52-72
Notes 73
Distribution of Communion 74-91
Notes 78
Laying hands anointing 92-93
Prayers for Protection and Peace 94-99
Marriage 101-193
Contents 101
Marriage 102-172
Pastoral Introduction 102
The Marriage Service 103-114
within Holy Communion 115-131
Notes 132-134
Supplementary texts 135-172
An Order for Prayer and Dedication after a Civil Marriage 173-183
Thanksgiving for Marriage 184-193
Emergency Baptism 195-198
See also CW Christian Initiation 102-105
Thanksgiving for the Gift of a Child 200-212
See also CW Christian Initiation 16-28 & the main volume 337-243
Funeral 214-415
Contents 214-215
Ministry at the Time of Death 216-235
Before the Funeral 236-254
The Funeral 255-317
Pastoral Introduction 256
Funeral Service 257-290
Notes 291-292
Supplementary texts 293-296
Funeral of Child 297-317
After the Funeral 318-344
At home 318
Burial of ashes 323-330
Memorials 331-344
Resources 345-415
Some only here
Alternative Services: Series One 417-460
Contents 417
Matrimony 418-429
Burial 430-460
Endmatter 462-478
General Rules 462
Authorization Details 463-464
Copyright Information 465
Acknowledgement of Sources 436-470
Index 471-478

6 New Patterns for Worship

The Church of England made a radical move in authorizing the Service of the Word in 1993 and then producing Patterns for Worship in 1995.

New Patterns for Worship is a revised edition of these resources as a part of Common Worship. It has also reworked the original material to be more than a resource book of prayers, but also to give directions to people on how to write their own material. This latter aspect, *Patterns* as a training resource, has perhaps been rather neglected.

The idea of a 'directory' of material came in 1985. This was further developed both as a response to the *Faith in the City* report being critical of the culture of the liturgical provision of the church, and also as a resource for the growing 'Family Service' movement. It was intended that there be a complete Communion rite included (Rite C); this is in part fulfilled by the Service of the Word with Holy Communion. However, the issue of eucharistic prayers with children has never been successfully resolved in Common Worship, some proposed prayers failing to get through General Synod in 1996.

The Service of the Word was at first an alternative form of service standing alongside the ASB. In Common Worship, the Service of the Word is the authorized provision for daily prayer. The Sunday forms in the main volume and those in *Common Worship: Daily Prayer* are commended examples of the Service of the Word. There is a very helpful section in *New Patterns* (pp 15–20) giving guidance on how to structure and compile a Service of the Word. This is essential reading for all involved in producing these services.

Text

The Archbishops' Council, *New Patterns for Worship* (London: CHP, 2002)

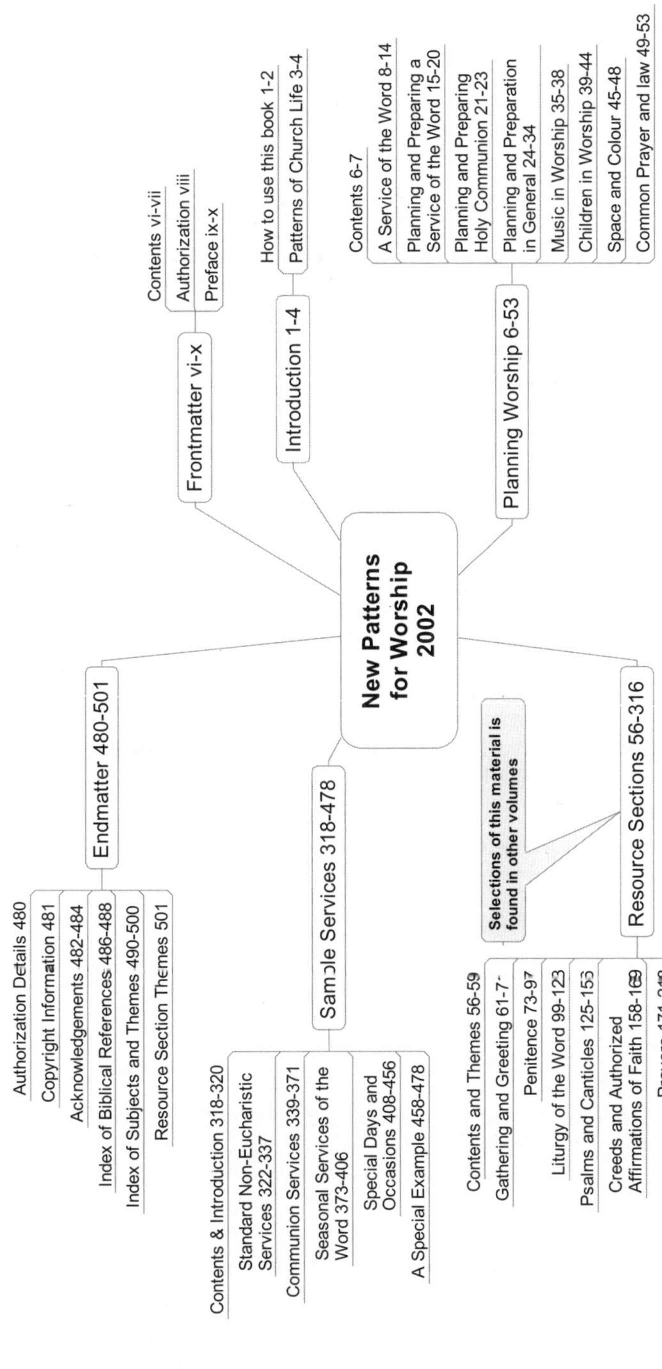
New Patterns for Worship 2002
Frontmatter vi-x
Contents vi-vii
Authorization viii
Preface ix-x
Introduction 1-4
How to use this book 1-2
Patterns of Church Life 3-4
Planning Worship 6-53
Contents 6-7
A Service of the Word 8-14
Planning and Preparing a Service of the Word 15-20
Planning and Preparing Holy Communion 21-23
Planning and Preparation in General 24-34
Music in Worship 35-38
Children in Worship 39-44
Space and Colour 45-48
Common Prayer and law 49-53
Endmatter 480-501
Authorization Details 480
Copyright Information 481
Acknowledgements 482-484
Index of Biblical References 486-488
Index of Subjects and Themes 490-500
Resource Section Themes 501
Sample Services 318-478
Contents & Introduction 318-320
Standard Non-Eucharistic Services 322-337
Communion Services 339-371
Seasonal Services of the Word 373-406
Special Days and Occasions 408-456
A Special Example 458-478
Resource Sections 56-316
Selections of this material is found in other volumes
Contents and Themes 56-59
Gathering and Greeting 61-71
Penitence 73-97
Liturgy of the Word 99-123
Psalms and Canticles 125-155
Creeds and Authorized Affirmations of Faith 158-169
Prayers 171-218
Praise and Thanksgiving 220-267
The Peace 269-277
Action and Movement 279-285
Conclusion 288-316

7 Daily Prayer

The present volume Daily Prayer is perhaps the richest provision of daily prayer material the Church of England has produced.

It has its roots in a collaboration project between members of the Liturgical Commission and the Society of St Francis (led by the late Br Tristram), to produce a new office book. In 1992 the popular *Celebrating Common Prayer* and *The Daily Office SSF* were produced. Technically this was a private production, even if it looked like an official book. In 2002 the Church of England produced *Daily Prayer Preliminary Edition*. This updated the provision in the areas of the calendar, psalter and a different approach to 'Prayer During the Day' to cover more informal daily prayer. In 2005 *Daily Prayer* was commended by the House of Bishops, ironing out some of the issues raised from the experience of using the Preliminary Edition. *Daily Prayer* is an outworking of the Service of the Word, which remains the authorized daily prayer provision of the Church.

Various offprints are now available of parts of the Book. A musical setting of Compline has been produced by the RSCM, and Prayer During the Day has been edited with Compline in one volume, *Time to Pray*. Volumes of spiritual readings have also been privately produced for holy and saints days, mostly to be used in daily prayer.

Texts

The Archbishops' Council, *Common Worship: Daily Prayer* (London: CHP, 2005)

The Archbishops' Council, *Time to Pray* (London: CHP, 2006)

J Harper (ed), *Music for Common Worship VI Night Prayer: Compline* (Dorking: RSCM, 2005)

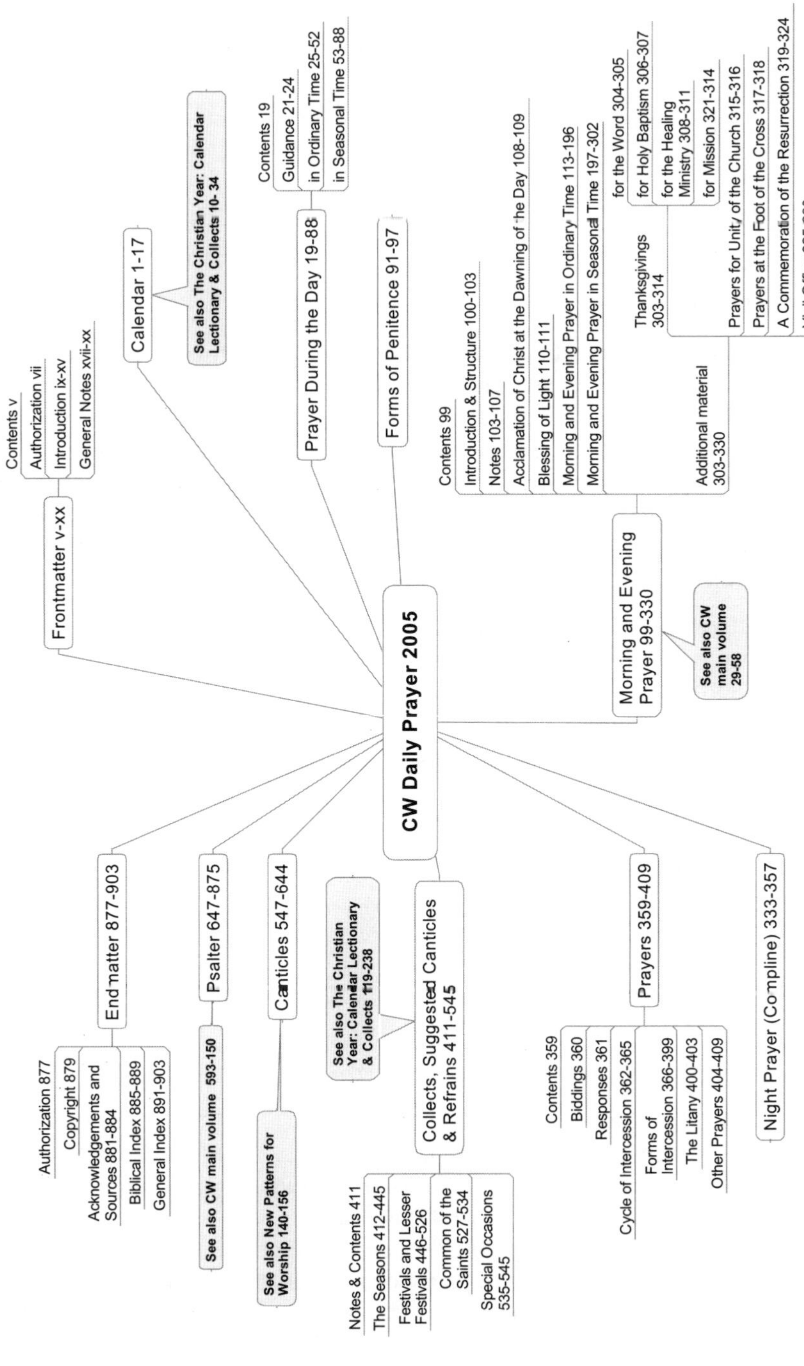
CW Daily Prayer 2005
Frontmatter v-xx
Contents v
Authorization vii
Introduction ix-xv
General Notes xvii-xx
Calendar 1-17
See also The Christian Year: Calendar Lectionary & Collects 10-34
Prayer During the Day 19-88
Contents 19
Guidance 21-24
in Ordinary Time 25-52
in Seasonal Time 53-88
Forms of Penitence 91-97
Morning and Evening Prayer 99-330
See also CW main volume 29-58
Contents 99
Introduction & Structure 100-103
Notes 103-107
Acclamation of Christ at the Dawning of the Day 108-109
Blessing of Light 110-111
Morning and Evening Prayer in Ordinary Time 113-196
Morning and Evening Prayer in Seasonal Time 197-302
Additional material 303-330
Thanksgivings 303-314
for the Word 304-305
for Holy Baptism 306-307
for the Healing Ministry 308-311
for Mission 321-314
Prayers for Unity of the Church 315-316
Prayers at the Foot of the Cross 317-318
A Commemoration of the Resurrection 319-324
Vigil Office 325-330
Night Prayer (Compline) 333-357
Prayers 359-409
Contents 359
Biddings 360
Responses 361
Cycle of Intercession 362-365
Forms of Intercession 366-399
The Litany 400-403
Other Prayers 404-409
Collects, Suggested Canticles & Refrains 411-545
See also The Christian Year: Calendar Lectionary & Collects 119-238
Notes & Contents 411
The Seasons 412-445
Festivals and Lesser Festivals 446-526
Common of the Saints 527-534
Special Occasions 535-545
Canticles 547-644
See also New Patterns for Worship 140-156
Psalter 647-875
See also CW main volume 593-150
End matter 877-903
Authorization 877
Copyright 879
Acknowledgements and Sources 881-884
Biblical Index 885-889
General Index 891-903

8 The Christian Year: Calendar, Lectionary and Collects

The calendar for Common Worship was produced before the main volume published in 1997. This has not changed since its publication.

The lectionary comes in three areas. The Sunday Lectionary is a Church of England amended version of the ecumenical Revised Common Lectionary. The Daily Eucharistic Lectionary is that of the Roman Catholic Church and has been used since the ASB as a Church of England Lectionary. A temporary weekday lectionary was introduced in 1999 and then changed in 2004. This is the present weekday lectionary provision. Almost everyone relies on the annually produced Lectionary book, where all the rules are applied and consolidated.

The collects were severely criticized and *Additional Collects* was produced in 2004. These have now been incorporated into the collect books. However, there are some collects (in traditional language) for saints' days only to be found in the *President's Edition.*

Texts

The Central Board of Finance of the Church of England, *The Christian Year: Calendar, Lectionary and Collects* (London: CHP, 1995, 1997)

The Archbishops' Council, *Common Worship: Additional Collects* (London: CHP, 2004)

The Archbishops' Council, *Common Worship: Collects and Post Communions* (London: CHP, 2004)

The Archbishops' Council, *Common Worship: Collects and Post Communions in Traditional Language* (London: CHP, 2004)

The General Synod of the Church of England, *Amendments to Calendar, Lectionary and Collects, and Rules for Regulating Authorized Forms of Service and to 'Rules to Order the Service and other Miscellaneous Liturgical Proposals'* (GS 1342A, as amended by GS 1342B, 2004), from www.cofe.anglican.org/worship/liturgy/commonworship/texts/lect/lectfront.html

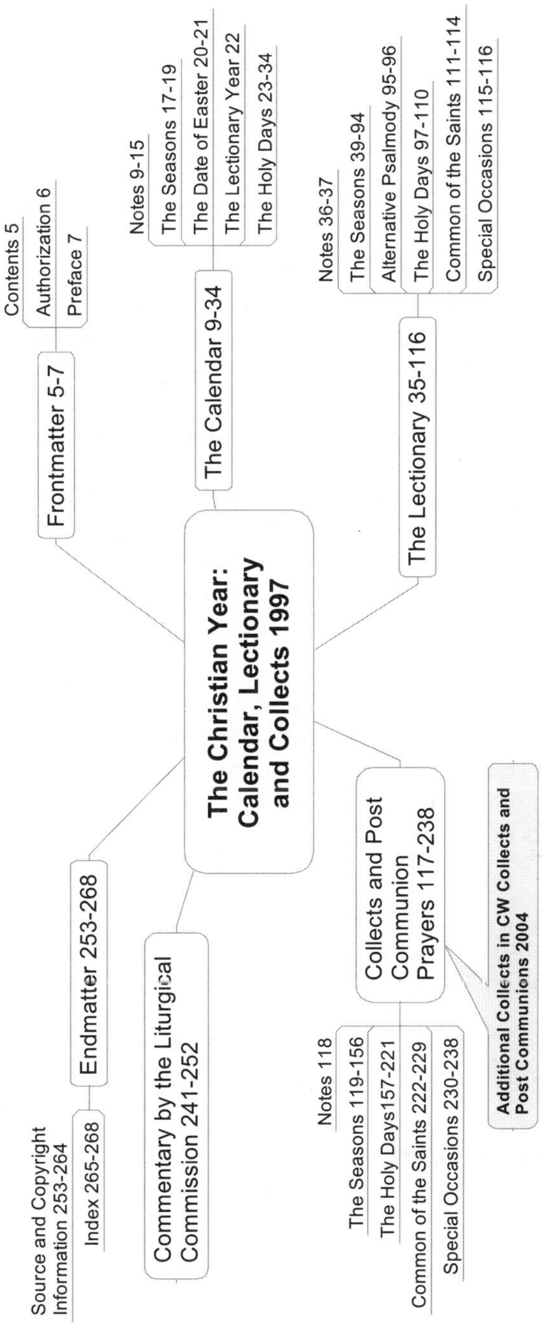

The Christian Year: Calendar, Lectionary and Collects 1997
Frontmatter 5-7
Contents 5
Authorization 6
Preface 7
The Calendar 9-34
Notes 9-15
The Seasons 17-19
The Date of Easter 20-21
The Lectionary Year 22
The Holy Days 23-34
The Lectionary 35-116
Notes 36-37
The Seasons 39-94
Alternative Psalmody 95-96
The Holy Days 97-110
Common of the Saints 111-114
Special Occasions 115-116
Collects and Post Communion Prayers 117-238
Notes 118
The Seasons 119-156
The Holy Days157-221
Common of the Saints 222-229
Special Occasions 230-238
Additional Collects in CW Collects and Post Communions 2004
Commentary by the Liturgical Commission 241-252
Endmatter 253-268
Source and Copyright Information 253-264
Index 265-268

9 Times and Seasons

The provision of seasonal material in the Church of England is quite recent in any volume.

There is the service of Commination in the *Book of Common Prayer*, and some additional services have at times been added, such as for King Charles the Martyr, also there has always been some scope for seasonal variation, but until recently the provision was minimalist. The official provision of copious seasonal material began in 1984 with the appearance of the popular *Lent Holy Week Easter*. This was followed up in 1991 with *The Promise of His Glory*, and supplemented by the unofficial 1993 *Enriching the Christian Year*. The desire with *Times and Seasons* was to draw all this together creating one volume of commended material for the Christian year. This has resulted in a very full book which concentrates more on material for Holy Communion and perhaps could have been better coordinated with *New Patterns for Worship*.

With such a large book this is one of the more complex maps. There is some overlap with other volumes in Common Worship but this is too complex to put on the chart and I refer those interested to pp 649–661 of the book. Imaginative use of the book should suggest that much of the material could be used in a variety of types of service. This is a resource book, rather than something to put in the hands of worshippers.

Texts

The Archbishops' Council, *Common Worship: Times and Seasons* (London: CHP, 2006)

Church of England, *Lent Holy Week Easter* (London: CHP, 1984, 1986)

Church of England, *The Promise of His Glory* (London: Mowbray/CHP, 1991)

M Perham (ed), *Enriching the Christian Year* (London: SPCK, 1992)

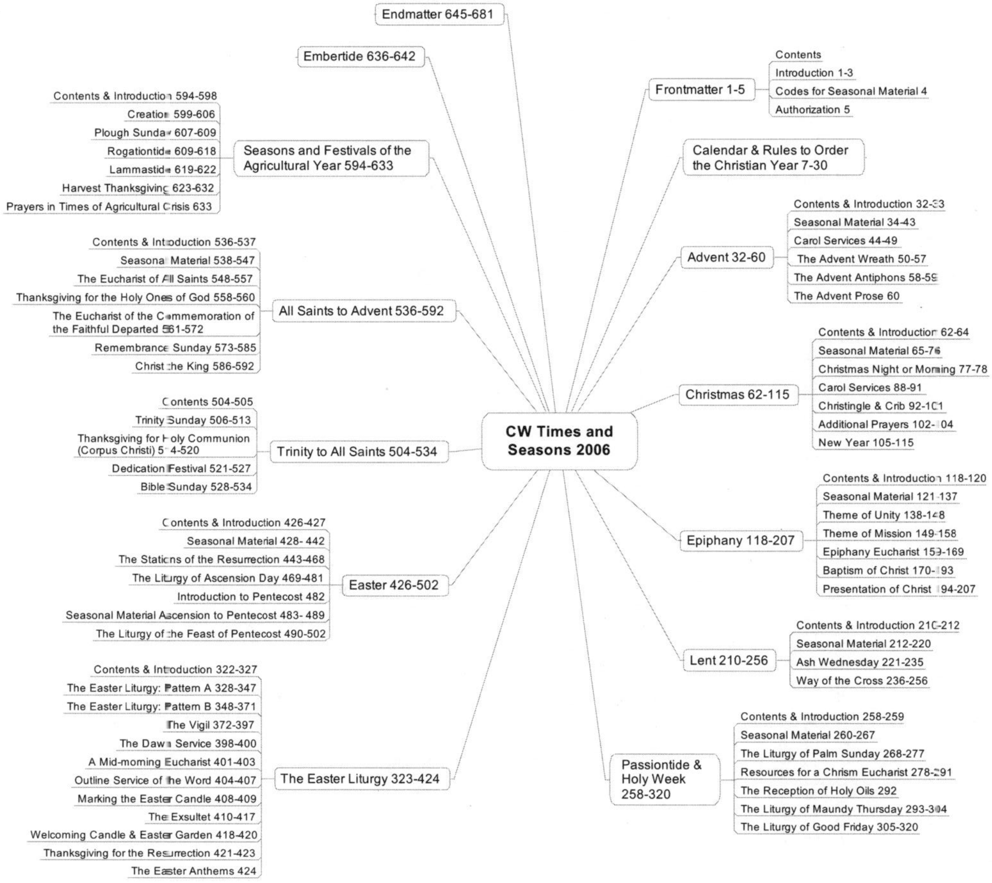
CW Times and Seasons 2006
Frontmatter 1-5
Contents
Introduction 1-3
Codes for Seasonal Material 4
Authorization 5
Calendar & Rules to Order the Christian Year 7-30
Advent 32-60
Contents & Introduction 32-33
Seasonal Material 34-43
Carol Services 44-49
The Advent Wreath 50-57
The Advent Antiphons 58-59
The Advent Prose 60
Christmas 62-115
Contents & Introduction 62-64
Seasonal Material 65-76
Christmas Night or Morning 77-78
Carol Services 88-91
Christingle & Crib 92-101
Additional Prayers 102-104
New Year 105-115
Epiphany 118-207
Contents & Introduction 118-120
Seasonal Material 121-137
Theme of Unity 138-148
Theme of Mission 149-158
Epiphany Eucharist 159-169
Baptism of Christ 170-193
Presentation of Christ 194-207
Lent 210-256
Contents & Introduction 210-212
Seasonal Material 212-220
Ash Wednesday 221-235
Way of the Cross 236-256
Passiontide & Holy Week 258-320
Contents & Introduction 258-259
Seasonal Material 260-267
The Liturgy of Palm Sunday 268-277
Resources for a Chrism Eucharist 278-291
The Reception of Holy Oils 292
The Liturgy of Maundy Thursday 293-304
The Liturgy of Good Friday 305-320
The Easter Liturgy 323-424
Contents & Introduction 322-327
The Easter Liturgy: Pattern A 328-347
The Easter Liturgy: Pattern B 348-371
The Vigil 372-397
The Dawn Service 398-400
A Mid-morning Eucharist 401-403
Outline Service of the Word 404-407
Marking the Easter Candle 408-409
The Exsultet 410-417
Welcoming Candle & Easter Garden 418-420
Thanksgiving for the Resurrection 421-423
The Easter Anthems 424
Easter 426-502
Contents & Introduction 426-427
Seasonal Material 428- 442
The Stations of the Resurrection 443-468
The Liturgy of Ascension Day 469-481
Introduction to Pentecost 482
Seasonal Material Ascension to Pentecost 483- 489
The Liturgy of the Feast of Pentecost 490-502
Trinity to All Saints 504-534
Contents 504-505
Trinity Sunday 506-513
Thanksgiving for Holy Communion (Corpus Christi) 514-520
Dedication Festival 521-527
Bible Sunday 528-534
All Saints to Advent 536-592
Contents & Introduction 536-537
Seasonal Material 538-547
The Eucharist of All Saints 548-557
Thanksgiving for the Holy Ones of God 558-560
The Eucharist of the Commemoration of the Faithful Departed 561-572
Remembrance Sunday 573-585
Christ the King 586-592
Seasons and Festivals of the Agricultural Year 594-633
Contents & Introduction 594-598
Creation 599-606
Plough Sunday 607-609
Rogationtide 609-618
Lammastide 619-622
Harvest Thanksgiving 623-632
Prayers in Times of Agricultural Crisis 633
Embertide 636-642
Endmatter 645-681

10 Festivals

Festivals is one of the final volumes of Common Worship to be produced.

It is published as a companion to *Times and Seasons*. It also includes any such material from 'the main book' as is necessary to lead the service of Holy Communion.

The book contains additional material for 29 festivals including the Annunciation, a principal feast day. These are mostly biblical saints or events. The additions to this are George, Day of Thanksgiving for the Institution of Holy Communion, and for a Dedication Festival. It also contains 'commons' for eight categories of saints' days and nine categories of special occasions. The book will be particularly useful for those churches that hold frequent services of Holy Communion and will be of particular use to the president.

Text

The Archbishops' Council, *Common Worship: Festivals* (London: CHP, 2008)

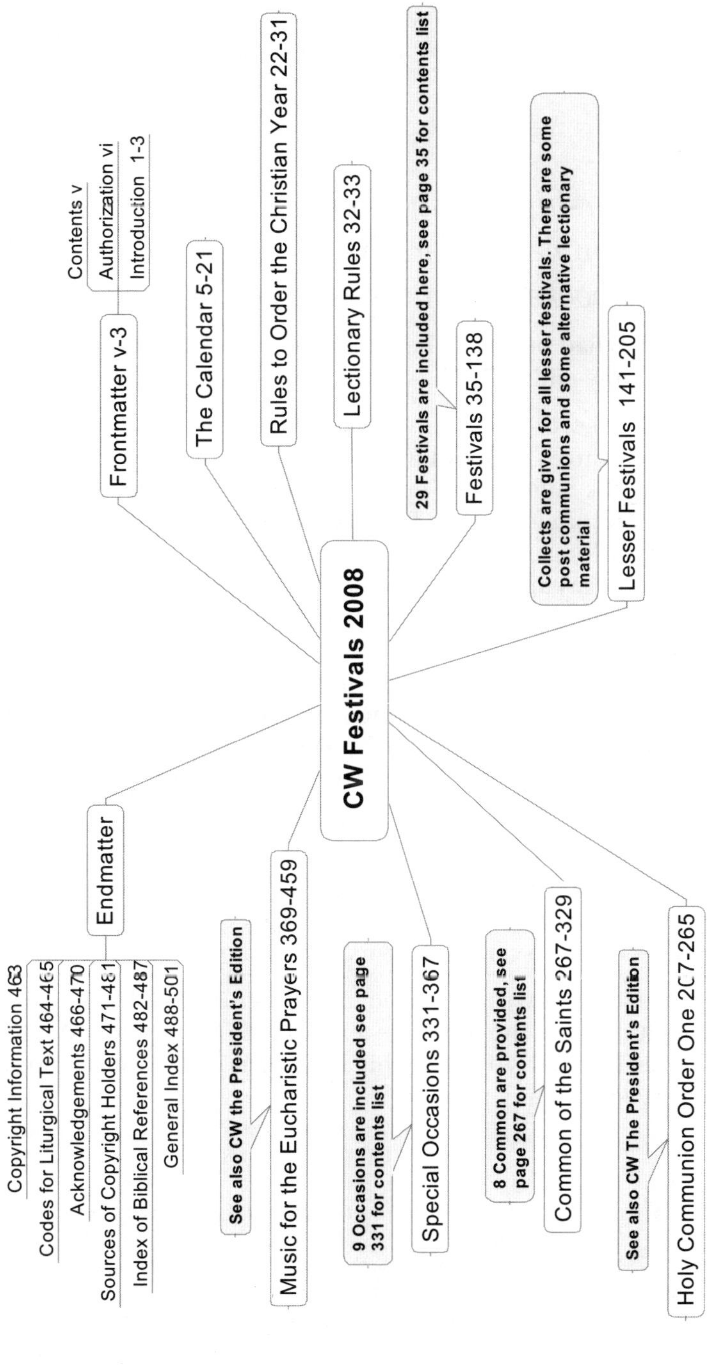
CW Festivals 2008
Frontmatter v-3
Contents v
Authorization vi
Introduction 1-3
The Calendar 5-21
Rules to Order the Christian Year 22-31
Lectionary Rules 32-33
Festivals 35-138
29 Festivals are included here, see page 35 for contents list
Lesser Festivals 141-205
Collects are given for all lesser festivals. There are some post communions and some alternative lectionary material
Holy Communion Order One 207-265
See also CW The President's Edition
Common of the Saints 267-329
8 Common are provided, see page 267 for contents list
Special Occasions 331-367
9 Occasions are included see page 331 for contents list
Music for the Eucharistic Prayers 369-459
See also CW the President's Edition
Endmatter
Copyright Information 463
Codes for Liturgical Text 464-465
Acknowledgements 466-470
Sources of Copyright Holders 471-481
Index of Biblical References 482-487
General Index 488-501

11 Ordination Services

Common Worship: Ordination Services is one of the last volumes to complete the original Common Worship idea, that of a series of books for contemporary worship.

The ASB ordinal had proved to be rather successful and its authorization was extended until the end of 2005.

Modern Anglican ordination services have their roots in the *Book of Common Worship* of the Church of South India. This re-emphasized the essence of ordination being the laying on of episcopal hands with prayer, rather than the medieval declaratory formulae. This was clearly expressed in the ASB, which reintroduced the long ordination prayer with a short formula in the middle of the prayer for the laying on of hands, of an invocation of the Spirit. Common Worship has tried to include two important emphases. The first is the mission context of ordination, which is not about elevating a person but shaping the church for mission. The second links to this in emphasizing that ministry is the function of the whole body of Christ and that ministers have a function in doing and shaping ministry, but they do not do it as the group that ministers in opposition to a group that receives ministry, the laity.

The shaping of the ordination services has been much influenced by the Inter Anglican Liturgical Consultations. This is the liturgy network of the ACC and the area of ordination has been a particularly significant aspect of their work. It is arguable that some of the most direct links on inter-Anglican thinking and Common Worship can be drawn at this point.

The text of the services was published in 2007 as a study edition with a number of essays included and the complete texts of the 1662 ordinal. While there are commentaries in other volumes, this has perhaps the most complete commentary provision of any volume.

Text

The Archbishops' Council, *Common Worship: Ordination Services Study Edition* (London: CHP)

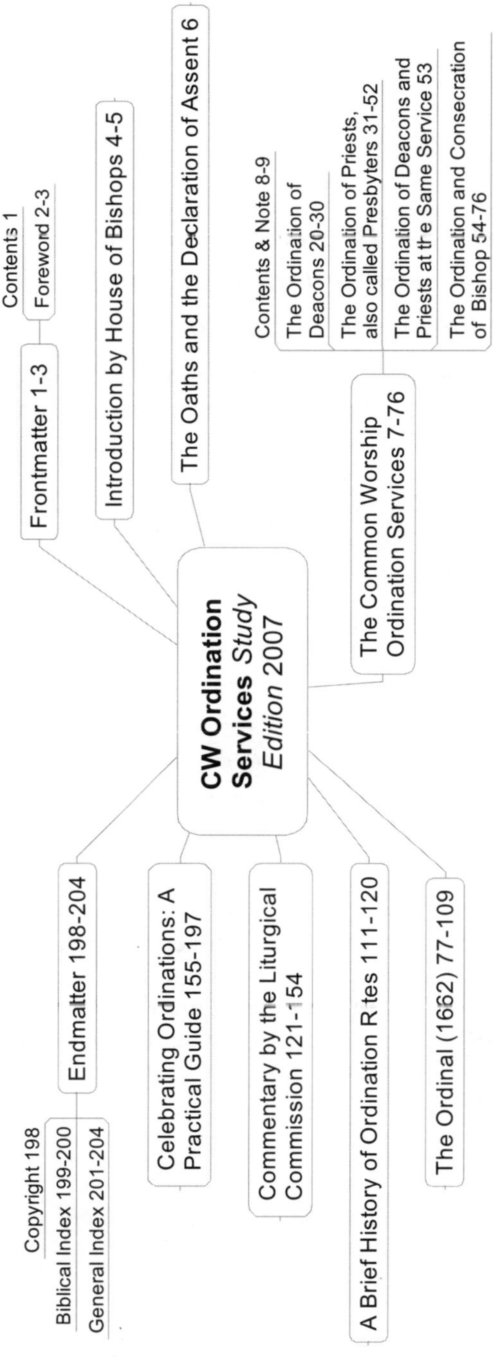
CW Ordination Services Study Edition 2007
Frontmatter 1-3
Contents 1
Foreword 2-3
Introduction by House of Bishops 4-5
The Oaths and the Declaration of Assent 6
The Common Worship Ordination Services 7-76
Contents & Note 8-9
The Ordination of Deacons 20-30
The Ordination of Priests, also called Presbyters 31-52
The Ordination of Deacons and Priests at the Same Service 53
The Ordination and Consecration of Bishop 54-76
The Ordinal (1662) 77-109
A Brief History of Ordination Rites 111-120
Commentary by the Liturgical Commission 121-154
Celebrating Ordinations: A Practical Guide 155-197
Endmatter 198-204
Copyright 198
Biblical Index 199-200
General Index 201-204

12 Other Services

This page includes two additional services in Common Worship and one service technically not a part of Common Worship but coming out of the same historical discussion.

The two texts are *Proclaiming the Passion* and *The Admission and Licensing of Readers*. The first presents the Passion narratives in dramatized form. This seems to have been omitted for *Times and Seasons* and is helpfully produced in this booklet. The second is a commended service, the first time of any national provision. It is to be welcomed that this has happened but unfortunate that it was not include in an episcopal book for other services such as admitting evangelists, dedicating churches, and celebrating 'religious' commitment.

Texts

The Archbishops' Council, *Proclaiming the Passion* (London: CHP, 2007)

The Archbishops' Council, *The Admission and Licensing of Readers* (London: CHP, 2007)

Public Worship with Communion by Extension (2001)

This is not an official Common Worship service; however, it is in Common Worship style using many of their texts. The service remains controversial, only just getting through General Synod. As a part of this process, it was agreed that this would not be included in the Common Worship volumes, particularly 'the main book.' Similar services are held in other Anglican Provinces, and the Roman Catholic Church has a Directory for 'Sunday Worship in the Absence of a Priest.'

Text

The Archbishops' Council, *Public Worship with Communion by Extension* (London: Church House Publishing, 2001)

Authorized but not in Common Worship

- Public Worship with Communion by Extension 2001
  - Notes v
  - General Notes vi
  - Order One 1-16
  - Order Two 17-30
  - Guidelines issued by House of Bishops 31-33
    - See also CW main volume 161-165
  - A Form of Preparation 35-39
  - General Rules 40
  - Authorization & Acknowledgements 41

Other Common Worship Services

- Proclaiming the Passion 2007
- The Admission and Licensing of Readers 2007

13 The Book of Common Prayer 1662

This chapter has been included for a number of reasons.

First to help clarify the difference between authorized and commended material and second to show the origins of some of the *Prayer Book* material included in Common Worship.

Any service that is alternative to the *Book of Common Prayer* has to be authorized by General Synod. This is the reason why lectionaries, ordinations, creeds, and eucharistic prayers were authorized by the Synod in producing Common Worship. However, material that is not found in the *Book of Common Prayer* such as crib services, memorial services, Compline, thanksgiving for the gift of a child, has been commended by the House of Bishops.

The *Book of Common Prayer* as we buy it today is not quite the same as the 1662 edition. Hence the map opposite has some sections in hexagonal boxes indicating their addition to the 1662 book. The services of the *Prayer Book* have been grouped using, where possible, terms from Common Worship to indicate the inter-relationship of the services. As there is no standardized pagination between various editions of the *Prayer Book*, so no page numbers have been added to the map.

Some parts of the Book of Common Prayer are found in Common Worship:

1. Morning and Evening Prayer—in the Main Volume
2. Prayers—Prayers from the Book of Common Prayer in the *Sunday Book*
3. The Litany—in the Main Volume
4. Collects—*Collects and Post Communions in Traditional Language*
5. Holy Communion—Order Two Holy Communion (adapted)
6. Canticles—From the *Book of Common Prayer* in the Main Volume
7. Consent and Vows—in the Marriage service.
8. The Ordinal—in Ordination Services

There is also material gathered from the *Book of Common Prayer* that has been adapted, not least to modern English, found in many of the volumes of Common Worship.

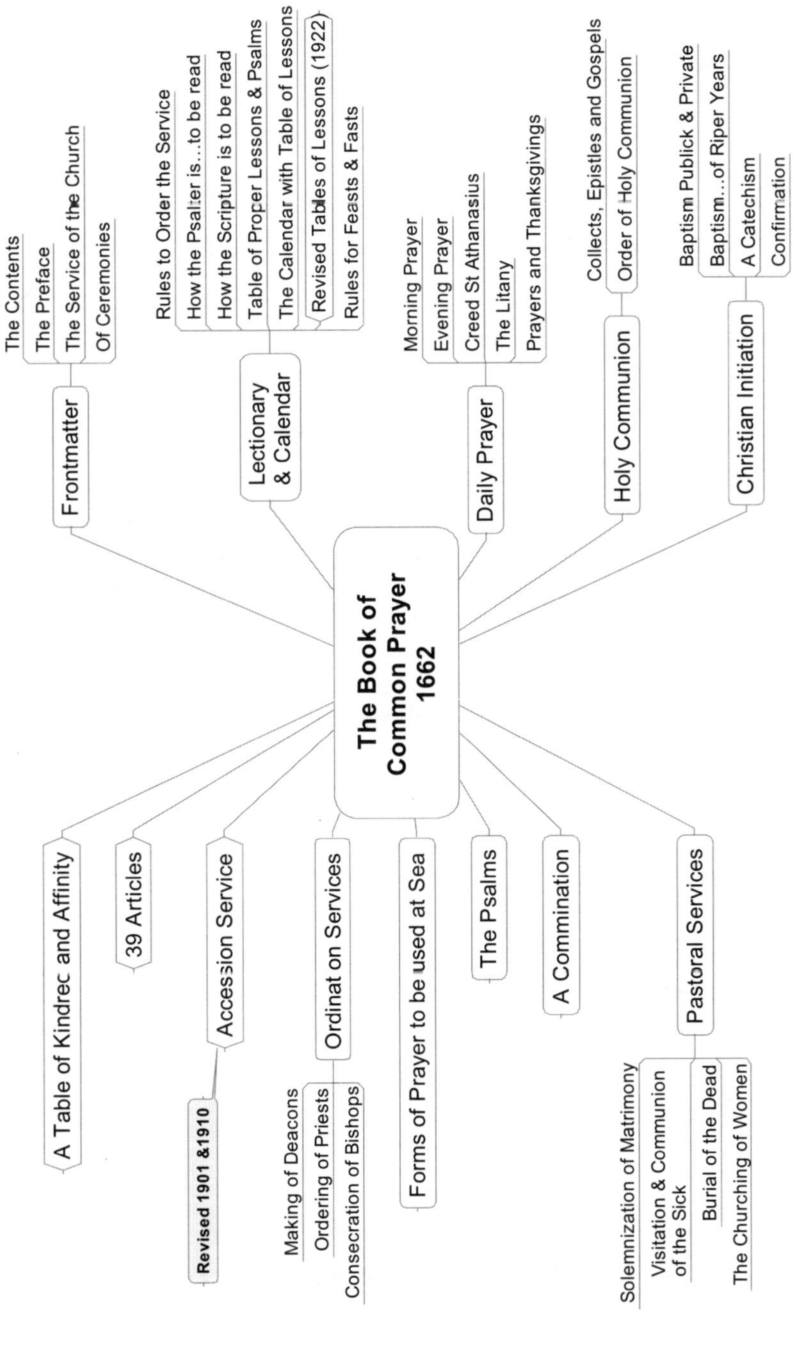
The Book of Common Prayer 1662
Frontmatter
The Contents
The Preface
The Service of the Church
Of Ceremonies
Lectionary & Calendar
Rules to Order the Service
How the Psalter is…to be read
How the Scripture is to be read
Table of Proper Lessons & Psalms
The Calendar with Table of Lessons
Revised Tables of Lessons (1922)
Rules for Feasts & Fasts
Daily Prayer
Morning Prayer
Evening Prayer
Creed St Athanasius
The Litany
Prayers and Thanksgivings
Holy Communion
Collects, Epistles and Gospels
Order of Holy Communion
Christian Initiation
Baptism Publick & Private
Baptism…of Riper Years
A Catechism
Confirmation
A Table of Kindred and Affinity
39 Articles
Accession Service
Revised 1901 &1910
Ordination Services
Making of Deacons
Ordering of Priests
Consecration of Bishops
Forms of Prayer to be used at Sea
The Psalms
A Commination
Pastoral Services
Solemnization of Matrimony
Visitation & Communion of the Sick
Burial of the Dead
The Churching of Women

14 Music

Various suggestions about music come up in some of the volumes for Common Worship, including places where there is musical notation.

Places where there is actual music include:

1 The *President's Edition,* including texts for singing the eucharistic prayers, pp 633–776, which can be downloaded from the Church of England website.

2 *New Patterns for Worship,* which includes sung responses, pp 179–180.

3 *Festivals* with music for eucharistic prefaces.

The report *In Tune with Heaven* (1992) set a new collaboration with various agencies for church music. The RSCM have been producing volumes of music for different Common Worship volumes, including a Psalter for Anglican chant. Sarum College have produced some musical resources for different services and Kevin Mayhew has also produced some resources. There is still much material that is not set to music including canticles for daily prayer, which is probably essential if they are to become used for more than for private reciting.

Psalter

A Moore, *Sunday Psalms: Musical Settings for Common Worship* (Stowmarket: Kevin Mayhew, 2000)

J Harper (ed), *The Common Worship Psalter with Chants* (Dorking: RSCM Press, 2002)

Notes

1 This is helped by the text being on the web and in *Visual Liturgy.*